First Line, Last Line

Jump-start Your Creative Writing
Volume 1

Suellen Williams

ISBN-13: 978-1499699760
ISBN-10: 149969976X

DEDICATION

for Seann and Baillie, a constant source of inspiration

CONTENTS

INTRODUCTION

A wise person once said that the best place to start is at the beginning. So, that is where I will start this booklet, at the beginning – the very first line. A memorable first line can be the difference between your writing standing out among the rest or fading into oblivion.

Throughout history there have been hundreds of novels that started with lines that are treasured even today. I do not profess that any of the lines I've penned here are even close to those historical literary standards, but then only time will tell. My best hope is that you will write the next best-selling novel based on my ideas. If not, I hope that one or more of them my get your creative juices flowing in the right direction.

I wrote this booklet with several kinds of people in mind.

To those suffering from writer's block,

Sometimes, starting is the hardest part of the creative writing process. Sometimes, you're stuck in the middle or near the end. Although there is no "sure fire" way to cure writer's block, there are ways that may help jump-start the creative process. Read through the first and last lines proposed in this book and maybe just one of them will take you to a place where you can get unstuck. Maybe you will come up with a new idea for a book or short story.

To those looking for story ideas,

Read through the ideas presented in the following pages and see if any of them appeal to you. Ask yourself why a book would start or end with the suggested lines. What is the story between the bookends?

To those hosting writers groups or teaching writing classes,

If you like a challenge, and most writers do, pick a random first line and/or a random last line and see what types of stories your group or class can come up with. It's amazing to see all the different directions a story can take, even when beginning from the same starting point.

I'm sure there are countless other ideas on how to use this book. What you get out of it is only limited by your imagination.

Enjoy!

Shall we begin?

FIRST LINES

1. A wise person once said that the best place to start is at the beginning.

2. She had procrastinated long enough.

3. Moving to Texas was a difficult decision.

4. He never thought he would win.

5. The phone call took her by surprise.

6. The circus was finally coming to Grove Creek.

7. I should have known better.

8. Lester was what they call a "good ol' boy".

9. We left in a hurry.

10. The sound was loud and persistent.

11. "Set sail."

12. Rachel looked up with a terrified expression.

13. If only I knew what he was thinking.

14. The wind carried it all away.

15. He could barley maintain his balance.

16. "Was that a fish?"

17. The key was old and tarnished.

18. William did not get what he deserved.

19. What does it mean to be a man?

20. Who would have believed me if I told the truth?

21. With spring came the torrential downpours.

22. Rudy dug into the frozen soil with his bare hands.

23. The stench was overwhelming.

24. It began with a loud, single blast.

25. The silence was broken by a sustained howl.

26. His dreams held no sound, only images.

27. She had just learned to stand on her own.

28. From a distance, he looked like a child.

29. Paisley drapes fluttered in the wind.

30. These are dangerous times.

31. Stuart Street was barricaded at dawn.

32. Information was the key to my success.

33. Arms and legs flailed about haphazardly.

34. Jessie's head was bursting with facts about _____.

35. We entered the stream from the south.

36. The signs were obvious.

37. Discontent is a powerful motivator.

38. After searching for four days, we finally found a signal.

39. It was an old family tradition.

40. Beverly was searching for rain clouds.

41. Wednesday promised to be delightfully boring.

42. How dare they!

43. The headline read like something out of a B-movie script.

44. "We don't get news out here."

45. After that day, eleven of us were never quite the same.

46. Nothing's as empty as a woman-less house.

47. She knew she had but one shot at this.

48. The shoreline was eroding quickly.

49. Speed was the ultimate goal.

50. The government was unaware of Mr. _____ and he preferred to keep it that way for now.

51. The dog was mangy and could not have been over six months old.

52. Insolence can be rewarding.

53. It took the me about ten seconds before I could place that face.

54. Keven was a picky eater right from Day 1.

55. The sparrows were watching Lulu as closely as she was watching them.

56. There is something that can learned from suffering but this is not it.

57. Try as I might, I couldn't get him to release it from his grip.

58. Thirty miles from Bakersville lies _____.

59. The Buddha made me do it.

60. Last week she could have named all of them.

61. I was 27 years old when the soldiers came.

62. Life can throw you a curve ball.

63. He needed to take a break.

64. They call me "Bubba" in an affectionate way.

65. I made bail and now I had some serious work to do.

66. "I used to be in a band."

67. I really screwed up this time.

68. I was there all night.

69. "I touched it and it fell apart."

70. He said I would be safe.

71. "Bless me, Father, for I have sinned."

72. I always looked up to him.

73. The ad promised unlimited wealth.

74. She never intended to be a foster-mother.

75. They would never figure out who started the brush fire.

76. I ran to the nearest store front hoping to avoid detection.

77. "That's just crazy talk."

78. It was a poor excuse for a tropical getaway.

79. Surely he won't recognize me.

80. It was not my cup of tea.

81. It sounded like such a great deal.

82. "We're moving to England!"

83. Everybody has one — it's the new thing.

84. We failed to remember Rule No. 1.

85. No one knows how this happened.

86. "I sure wasn't expecting this."

87. The cargo ship arrived in Bangor with no time to spare.

88. My greatest flaw is that I over-think everything.

89. "I think we got off on the wrong foot."

90. Sara sat quietly and awaited their decision.

91. "You'll never see me again," he said as he headed toward Corpus Christi.

92. Who did he think he was dealing with?

93. It's as plain as the nose on your face.

94. "You'll never take me alive."

95. She had to remind herself not to blush as she read the report.

96. It's time for a new _____.

97. I'm not really the chatty type but _____.

98. It was smooth and glowing.

99. His real name was Micheal Duffy.

100. I never told this to anyone, until now.

LAST LINES

1. That's when it hit him.

2. There was no one to blame but myself.

3. She picked up the check and left.

4. After all, a promise is a promise.

5. I should have listened to my mother.

6. So, this is paradise.

7. It ended just as it had begun.

8. Pirate treasure! No way.

9. He could stand up but refused to.

10. Then everything turned blue.

11. I now call that river valley home.

12. She danced until she cried.

13. "Seriously?"

14. The race is on.

15. If I could sing, I would.

16. "I'm ready when you are."

17. If I had known the stories surrounding the bridge, I never would have boarded that train.

18. ... and that's the least of my worries.

19. Snow kept falling measuring feet, not inches, and I didn't care if it ever stopped.

20. Her dream took her right to the edge.

21. Dawn never came.

22. At last, I was free.

23. "You may remain silent."

24. All we could do was dance.

25. "Go ahead. Take my picture."

26. My gambling days are over.

27. "I know nothing."

28. I had this one chance and I blew it.

29. I cut up the credit card.

30. Anything less would have been unacceptable.

31. "Anyone care for some tea?"

32. "Promise me you won't tell a soul."

33. I swear this is God's truth.

34. Never again.

35. Now they're talking.

36. That's how a ride became a journey.

37. It's valet parking from now on.

38. "This is wonderful news."

39. She didn't trust herself one bit.

40. ... 25 year old, single malt.

41. I have my own theory on that.

42. She never saw it coming.

43. I'm one step ahead again.

44. "That's my story and I'm sticking to it."

45. "Sinatra was the best", he argued.

46. Remember me fondly.

47. She was left with a song in her heart.

48. I guess they were trying to tell us something.

49. It's never really the end.

50. In fact, the sun rose like always.

51. Pass it on.

52. "No _____ for you!"

53. I'll never look at _____ in that way again.

54. Sad but true.

55. "That was a fine mess you got us into."

56. There's plenty more where that came from.

57. Then I saw him cross the road.

58. She had it all figured out.

59. "I'm going to ask you one more time."

60. Silence.

61. They found her in Canada.

62. I've never had an interest in going to China anyway.

63. Tough day!

64. I hope he understands.

65. We made a good team.

66. Guilty as charged.

67. That's how I came to be known as "Bubba".

68. "Daddy, is this really the end?"

69. Only time will tell.

70. Are you impressed?

71. It couldn't have been any more toxic.

72. I donated the rest.

73. Granted, it saved some time but it wasn't worth the price.

74. Not a good time for a brain fart!

75. Sweet revenge.

76. "I'll take two."

77. That's how this all became public information.

78. You don't need to know the rest of it.

79. "Speak of the devil."

80. It really was a big deal.

81. They don't do it like that in Texas.

82. I couldn't have planned it better myself.

83. Thus begins the next revolution.

84. "I think we're done here."

85. So, I learned to live with it in silence.

86. It all seemed so real.

87. I may have crossed the line between confident and cocky.

88. "I'll take it."

89. The house filled with laughter.

90. "I know what side my bread is buttered on."

91. Only ten more to go.

92. I hate trickery in any form.

93. What an unexpected pleasure.

94. And so it ends happily, like all good tales.

95. It was no joking matter.

96. I got in line and walked with the rest of them.

97. It's not always about me.

98. Breakfast is still my favorite meal.

99. It was the biggest gathering in all of Walnut Creek.

100. Shall we begin?

FAMOUS FIRST LINES

The American Book Review, School of Arts & Sciences, has identified the 100 Best First Lines from Novels. Who knows? One day, you may make this list.

1.   Call me Ishmael. —Herman Melville, Moby-Dick (1851)

2.   It is a truth universally acknowledged, that a single man in possession of a good fortune, must be in want of a wife. —Jane Austen, Pride and Prejudice (1813)

3.   A screaming comes across the sky. —Thomas Pynchon, Gravity's Rainbow (1973)

4.   Many years later, as he faced the firing squad, Colonel Aureliano Buendía was to remember that distant afternoon when his father took him to discover ice. —Gabriel García Márquez, One Hundred Years of Solitude (1967; trans. Gregory Rabassa)

5.   Lolita, light of my life, fire of my loins. —Vladimir Nabokov, Lolita (1955)

6. Happy families are all alike; every unhappy family is unhappy in its own way. —Leo Tolstoy, Anna Karenina (1877; trans. Constance Garnett)

7. riverrun, past Eve and Adam's, from swerve of shore to bend of bay, brings us by a commodius vicus of recirculation back to Howth Castle and Environs. —James Joyce, Finnegans Wake (1939)

8. It was a bright cold day in April, and the clocks were striking thirteen. —George Orwell, 1984 (1949)

9. It was the best of times, it was the worst of times, it was the age of wisdom, it was the age of foolishness, it was the epoch of belief, it was the epoch of incredulity, it was the season of Light, it was the season of Darkness, it was the spring of hope, it was the winter of despair. —Charles Dickens, A Tale of Two Cities (1859)

10. I am an invisible man. —Ralph Ellison, Invisible Man (1952)

11. The Miss Lonelyhearts of the New York Post-Dispatch (Are you in trouble?—Do-you-need-advice?—Write-to-Miss-Lonelyhearts-and-she-will-help-you) sat at his desk and stared at a piece of white cardboard. —Nathanael West, Miss Lonelyhearts (1933)

12. You don't know about me without you have read a book by the name of The Adventures of Tom Sawyer; but that ain't no matter. —Mark Twain, Adventures of Huckleberry Finn (1885)

13. Someone must have slandered Josef K., for one morning, without having done anything truly wrong, he was arrested. —Franz Kafka, The Trial (1925; trans. Breon Mitchell)

14. You are about to begin reading Italo Calvino's new novel, If on a winter's night a traveler. —Italo Calvino, *If on a winter's night a traveler* (1979; trans. William Weaver)

15. The sun shone, having no alternative, on the nothing new. —Samuel Beckett, *Murphy* (1938)

16. If you really want to hear about it, the first thing you'll probably want to know is where I was born, and what my lousy childhood was like, and how my parents were occupied and all before they had me, and all that David Copperfield kind of crap, but I don't feel like going into it, if you want to know the truth. —J. D. Salinger, *The Catcher in the Rye* (1951)

17. Once upon a time and a very good time it was there was a moocow coming down along the road and this moocow that was coming down along the road met a nicens little boy named baby tuckoo. —James Joyce, *A Portrait of the Artist as a Young Man* (1916)

18. This is the saddest story I have ever heard. —Ford Madox Ford, *The Good Soldier* (1915)

19. I wish either my father or my mother, or indeed both of them, as they were in duty both equally bound to it, had minded what they were about when they begot me; had they duly considered how much depended upon what they were then doing;—that not only the production of a rational Being was concerned in it, but that possibly the happy formation and temperature of his body, perhaps his genius and the very cast of his mind;—and, for aught they knew to the contrary, even the fortunes of his whole house might take their turn from the humours and dispositions which were then uppermost:—Had they duly weighed and considered all this, and proceeded accordingly,—I am verily persuaded I should have made a quite different figure in the world, from that, in which the reader is likely to see me. —Laurence Sterne, Tristram Shandy (1759–1767)

20. Whether I shall turn out to be the hero of my own life, or whether that station will be held by anybody else, these pages must show. —Charles Dickens, David Copperfield (1850)

21. Stately, plump Buck Mulligan came from the stairhead, bearing a bowl of lather on which a mirror and a razor lay crossed. —James Joyce, Ulysses (1922)

22. It was a dark and stormy night; the rain fell in torrents, except at occasional intervals, when it was checked by a violent gust of wind which swept up the streets (for it is in London that our scene lies), rattling along the house-tops, and fiercely agitating the scanty flame of the lamps that struggled against the darkness. —Edward George Bulwer-Lytton, Paul Clifford (1830)

23. One summer afternoon Mrs. Oedipa Maas came home from a Tupperware party whose hostess had put perhaps too much kirsch in the fondue to find that she, Oedipa, had been named executor, or she supposed executrix, of the estate of one Pierce Inverarity, a California real estate mogul who had once lost two million dollars in his spare time but still had assets numerous and tangled enough to make the job of sorting it all out more than honorary. —Thomas Pynchon, The Crying of Lot 49 (1966)

24. It was a wrong number that started it, the telephone ringing three times in the dead of night, and the voice on the other end asking for someone he was not. —Paul Auster, City of Glass (1985)

25. Through the fence, between the curling flower spaces, I could see them hitting. —William Faulkner, The Sound and the Fury (1929)

26. 124 was spiteful. —Toni Morrison, Beloved (1987)

27. Somewhere in la Mancha, in a place whose name I do not care to remember, a gentleman lived not long ago, one of those who has a lance and ancient shield on a shelf and keeps a skinny nag and a greyhound for racing. —Miguel de Cervantes, Don Quixote (1605; trans. Edith Grossman)

28. Mother died today. —Albert Camus, The Stranger (1942; trans. Stuart Gilbert)

29. Every summer Lin Kong returned to Goose Village to divorce his wife, Shuyu. —Ha Jin, Waiting (1999)

30. The sky above the port was the color of television, tuned to a dead channel. —William Gibson, Neuromancer (1984)

31. I am a sick man . . . I am a spiteful man. —Fyodor Dostoyevsky, Notes from Underground (1864; trans. Michael R. Katz)

32. Where now? Who now? When now? —Samuel Beckett, The Unnamable (1953; trans. Patrick Bowles)

33. Once an angry man dragged his father along the ground through his own orchard. "Stop!" cried the groaning old man at last, "Stop! I did not drag my father beyond this tree." —Gertrude Stein, The Making of Americans (1925)

34. In a sense, I am Jacob Horner. —John Barth, The End of the Road (1958)

35. It was like so, but wasn't. —Richard Powers, Galatea 2.2 (1995)

36. —Money . . . in a voice that rustled. —William Gaddis, J R (1975)

37. Mrs. Dalloway said she would buy the flowers herself. — Virginia Woolf, Mrs. Dalloway (1925)

38. All this happened, more or less. —Kurt Vonnegut, Slaughterhouse-Five (1969)

39. They shoot the white girl first. —Toni Morrison, Paradise (1998)

40. For a long time, I went to bed early. —Marcel Proust, Swann's Way (1913; trans. Lydia Davis)

41. The moment one learns English, complications set in. — Felipe Alfau, Chromos (1990)

42. Dr. Weiss, at forty, knew that her life had been ruined by literature. —Anita Brookner, The Debut (1981)

43. I was the shadow of the waxwing slain / By the false azure in the windowpane; —Vladimir Nabokov, Pale Fire (1962)

44. Ships at a distance have every man's wish on board. —Zora Neale Hurston, Their Eyes Were Watching God (1937)

45. I had the story, bit by bit, from various people, and, as generally happens in such cases, each time it was a different story. —Edith Wharton, Ethan Frome (1911)

46. Ages ago, Alex, Allen and Alva arrived at Antibes, and Alva allowing all, allowing anyone, against Alex's admonition, against Allen's angry assertion: another African amusement . . . anyhow, as all argued, an awesome African army assembled and arduously advanced against an African anthill, assiduously annihilating ant after ant, and afterward, Alex astonishingly accuses Albert as also accepting Africa's antipodal ant annexation. —Walter Abish, Alphabetical Africa (1974)

47. There was a boy called Eustace Clarence Scrubb, and he almost deserved it. —C. S. Lewis, The Voyage of the Dawn Treader (1952)

48. He was an old man who fished alone in a skiff in the Gulf Stream and he had gone eighty-four days now without taking a fish. —Ernest Hemingway, The Old Man and the Sea (1952)

49. It was the day my grandmother exploded. —Iain M. Banks, The Crow Road (1992)

50. I was born twice: first, as a baby girl, on a remarkably smogless Detroit day in January of 1960; and then again, as a teenage boy, in an emergency room near Petoskey, Michigan, in August of 1974. —Jeffrey Eugenides, Middlesex (2002)

51. Elmer Gantry was drunk. —Sinclair Lewis, Elmer Gantry (1927)

52. We started dying before the snow, and like the snow, we continued to fall. —Louise Erdrich, Tracks (1988)

53. It was a pleasure to burn. —Ray Bradbury, Fahrenheit 451 (1953)

54. A story has no beginning or end; arbitrarily one chooses that moment of experience from which to look back or from which to look ahead. —Graham Greene, The End of the Affair (1951)

55. Having placed in my mouth sufficient bread for three minutes' chewing, I withdrew my powers of sensual perception and retired into the privacy of my mind, my eyes and face assuming a vacant and preoccupied expression. —Flann O'Brien, At Swim-Two-Birds (1939)

56. I was born in the Year 1632, in the City of York, of a good Family, tho' not of that Country, my Father being a Foreigner of Bremen, who settled first at Hull; He got a good Estate by Merchandise, and leaving off his Trade, lived afterward at York, from whence he had married my Mother, whose Relations were named Robinson, a very good Family in that Country, and from whom I was called Robinson Kreutznaer; but by the usual Corruption of Words in England, we are now called, nay we call our selves, and write our Name Crusoe, and so my Companions always call'd me. —Daniel Defoe, Robinson Crusoe (1719)

57. In the beginning, sometimes I left messages in the street. —David Markson, Wittgenstein's Mistress (1988)

58. Miss Brooke had that kind of beauty which seems to be thrown into relief by poor dress. —George Eliot, Middlemarch (1872)

59. It was love at first sight. —Joseph Heller, Catch-22 (1961)

60. What if this young woman, who writes such bad poems, in competition with her husband, whose poems are equally bad, should stretch her remarkably long and well-made legs out before you, so that her skirt slips up to the tops of her stockings? —Gilbert Sorrentino, Imaginative Qualities of Actual Things (1971)

61. I have never begun a novel with more misgiving. —W. Somerset Maugham, The Razor's Edge (1944)

62. Once upon a time, there was a woman who discovered she had turned into the wrong person. —Anne Tyler, Back When We Were Grownups (2001)

63. The human race, to which so many of my readers belong, has been playing at children's games from the beginning, and will probably do it till the end, which is a nuisance for the few people who grow up. —G. K. Chesterton, The Napoleon of Notting Hill (1904)

64. In my younger and more vulnerable years my father gave me some advice that I've been turning over in my mind ever since. —F. Scott Fitzgerald, The Great Gatsby (1925)

65. You better not never tell nobody but God. —Alice Walker, The Color Purple (1982)

66. "To be born again," sang Gibreel Farishta tumbling from the heavens, "first you have to die." —Salman Rushdie, The Satanic Verses (1988)

67. It was a queer, sultry summer, the summer they electrocuted the Rosenbergs, and I didn't know what I was doing in New York. —Sylvia Plath, The Bell Jar (1963)

68. Most really pretty girls have pretty ugly feet, and so does Mindy Metalman, Lenore notices, all of a sudden. —David Foster Wallace, The Broom of the System (1987)

69. If I am out of my mind, it's all right with me, thought Moses Herzog. —Saul Bellow, Herzog (1964)

70. Francis Marion Tarwater's uncle had been dead for only half a day when the boy got too drunk to finish digging his grave and a Negro named Buford Munson, who had come to get a jug filled, had to finish it and drag the body from the breakfast table where it was still sitting and bury it in a decent and Christian way, with the sign of its Saviour at the head of the grave and enough dirt on top to keep the dogs from digging it up. —Flannery O'Connor, The Violent Bear it Away (1960)

71. Granted: I am an inmate of a mental hospital; my keeper is watching me, he never lets me out of his sight; there's a peephole in the door, and my keeper's eye is the shade of brown that can never see through a blue-eyed type like me. —GŸnter Grass, The Tin Drum (1959; trans. Ralph Manheim)

72. When Dick Gibson was a little boy he was not Dick Gibson. —Stanley Elkin, The Dick Gibson Show (1971)

73. Hiram Clegg, together with his wife Emma and four friends of the faith from Randolph Junction, were summoned by the Spirit and Mrs. Clara Collins, widow of the beloved Nazarene preacher Ely Collins, to West Condon on the weekend of the eighteenth and nineteenth of April, there to await the End of the World. —Robert Coover, The Origin of the Brunists (1966)

74. She waited, Kate Croy, for her father to come in, but he kept her unconscionably, and there were moments at which she showed herself, in the glass over the mantel, a face positively pale with the irritation that had brought her to the point of going away without sight of him. —Henry James, The Wings of the Dove (1902)

75. In the late summer of that year we lived in a house in a village that looked across the river and the plain to the mountains. —Ernest Hemingway, A Farewell to Arms (1929)

76. "Take my camel, dear," said my Aunt Dot, as she climbed down from this animal on her return from High Mass. — Rose Macaulay, The Towers of Trebizond (1956)

77. He was an inch, perhaps two, under six feet, powerfully built, and he advanced straight at you with a slight stoop of the shoulders, head forward, and a fixed from-under stare which made you think of a charging bull. —Joseph Conrad, Lord Jim (1900)

78. The past is a foreign country; they do things differently there. —L. P. Hartley, The Go-Between (1953)

79. On my naming day when I come 12 I gone front spear and kilt a wyld boar he parbly ben the las wyld pig on the Bundel Downs any how there hadnt ben none for a long time befor him nor I aint looking to see none agen. —Russell Hoban, Riddley Walker (1980)

80. Justice?—You get justice in the next world, in this world you have the law. —William Gaddis, A Frolic of His Own (1994)

81. Vaughan died yesterday in his last car-crash. —J. G. Ballard, Crash (1973)

82. I write this sitting in the kitchen sink. —Dodie Smith, I Capture the Castle (1948)

83. "When your mama was the geek, my dreamlets," Papa would say, "she made the nipping off of noggins such a crystal mystery that the hens themselves yearned toward her, waltzing around her, hypnotized with longing." —Katherine Dunn, Geek Love (1983)

84. In the last years of the Seventeenth Century there was to be found among the fops and fools of the London coffee-houses one rangy, gangling flitch called Ebenezer Cooke, more ambitious than talented, and yet more talented than prudent, who, like his friends-in-folly, all of whom were supposed to be educating at Oxford or Cambridge, had found the sound of Mother English more fun to game with than her sense to labor over, and so rather than applying himself to the pains of scholarship, had learned the knack of versifying, and ground out quires of couplets after the fashion of the day, afroth with Joves and Jupiters, aclang with jarring rhymes, and string-taut with similes stretched to the snapping-point. —John Barth, The Sot-Weed Factor (1960)

85. When I finally caught up with Abraham Trahearne, he was drinking beer with an alcoholic bulldog named Fireball Roberts in a ramshackle joint just outside of Sonoma, California, drinking the heart right out of a fine spring afternoon. —James Crumley, The Last Good Kiss (1978)

86. It was just noon that Sunday morning when the sheriff reached the jail with Lucas Beauchamp though the whole town (the whole county too for that matter) had known since the night before that Lucas had killed a white man. —William Faulkner, Intruder in the Dust (1948)

87. I, Tiberius Claudius Drusus Nero Germanicus This-that-and-the-other (for I shall not trouble you yet with all my titles) who was once, and not so long ago either, known to my friends and relatives and associates as "Claudius the Idiot," or "That Claudius," or "Claudius the Stammerer," or "Clau-Clau-Claudius" or at best as "Poor Uncle Claudius," am now about to write this strange history of my life; starting from my earliest childhood and continuing year by year until I reach the fateful point of change where, some eight years ago, at the age of fifty-one, I suddenly found myself caught in what I may call the "golden predicament" from which I have never since become disentangled. —Robert Graves, I, Claudius (1934)

88. Of all the things that drive men to sea, the most common disaster, I've come to learn, is women. —Charles Johnson, Middle Passage (1990)

89. I am an American, Chicago born—Chicago, that somber city—and go at things as I have taught myself, free-style, and will make the record in my own way: first to knock, first admitted; sometimes an innocent knock, sometimes a not so innocent. —Saul Bellow, The Adventures of Augie March (1953)

90. The towers of Zenith aspired above the morning mist; austere towers of steel and cement and limestone, sturdy as cliffs and delicate as silver rods. —Sinclair Lewis, Babbitt (1922)

91. I will tell you in a few words who I am: lover of the hummingbird that darts to the flower beyond the rotted sill where my feet are propped; lover of bright needlepoint and the bright stitching fingers of humorless old ladies bent to their sweet and infamous designs; lover of parasols made from the same puffy stuff as a young girl's underdrawers; still lover of that small naval boat which somehow survived the distressing years of my life between her decks or in her pilothouse; and also lover of poor dear black Sonny, my mess boy, fellow victim and confidant, and of my wife and child. But most of all, lover of my harmless and sanguine self. —John Hawkes, Second Skin (1964)

92. He was born with a gift of laughter and a sense that the world was mad. —Raphael Sabatini, Scaramouche (1921)

93. Psychics can see the color of time it's blue. —Ronald Sukenick, Blown Away (1986)

94. In the town, there were two mutes and they were always together. —Carson McCullers, The Heart is a Lonely Hunter (1940)

95. Time is not a line but a dimension, like the dimensions of space. —Margaret Atwood, Cat's Eye (1988)

96. He—for there could be no doubt of his sex, though the fashion of the time did something to disguise it—was in the act of slicing at the head of a Moor which swung from the rafters. —Virginia Woolf, Orlando (1928)

97. High, high above the North Pole, on the first day of 1969, two professors of English Literature approached each other at a combined velocity of 1200 miles per hour. —David Lodge, Changing Places (1975)

98. They say when trouble comes close ranks, and so the white people did. —Jean Rhys, Wide Sargasso Sea (1966)

99. The cold passed reluctantly from the earth, and the retiring fogs revealed an army stretched out on the hills, resting. —Stephen Crane, The Red Badge of Courage (1895

100.Once upon a time two or three weeks ago, a rather stubborn and determined middle-aged man decided to record for posterity, exactly as it happened, word by word and step by step, the story of another man for indeed what is great in man is that he is a bridge and not a goal, a somewhat paranoiac fellow unmarried, unattached, and quite irresponsible, who had decided to lock himself in a room a furnished room with a private bath, cooking facilities, a bed, a table, and at least one chair, in New York City, for a year 365 days to be precise, to write the story of another person—a shy young man about of 19 years old— who, after the war the Second World War, had come to America the land of opportunities from France under the sponsorship of his uncle—a journalist, fluent in five languages—who himself had come to America from Europe Poland it seems, though this was not clearly established sometime during the war after a series of rather gruesome adventures, and who, at the end of the war, wrote to the father his cousin by marriage of the young man whom he considered as a nephew, curious to know if he the father and his family had survived the German occupation, and indeed was deeply saddened to learn, in a letter from the young man—a long and touching letter written in English, not by the young man, however, who did not know a damn word of English, but by a good friend of his who had studied English in school—that his parents both his father and mother and his two sisters one older and the other younger than he had been deported they were Jewish to a German concentration camp Auschwitz probably and never returned, no doubt having been exterminated deliberately X * X * X * X, and that, therefore, the young man who was now an orphan, a displaced person, who, during the war, had managed to escape deportation by working very hard on a farm in Southern France, would be happy and grateful to be given the opportunity to come to America that great country he had heard so much about and yet knew so little about to start a new life, possibly go to school, learn a trade, and become a good, loyal citizen. —Raymond Federman, Double or Nothing (1971)

ABOUT THE AUTHOR

Suellen Williams is "a riddle wrapped in a mystery inside an enigma". Not really but it's a great line. It was funny when Winston Churchill said it a radio broadcast in October 1939 and it's still funny today.

Suellen spends most of her time deep in thought – scheming and planning her next book, story, tutorial – anything to keep the old brain nimble and quick.

For those who just "need to know" she can be described as a:

mom
daughter
sister
wife
grandmother
Florida resident
sports fan (Go Blue!)
Detroit raised (Go Wings!)
all-around good ol' gal

CREATIVE WRITING SERIES

First Line, Last Line
Jump-start Your Creative Writing
Volume 1
June 2014

www.ingramcontent.com/pod-product-compliance
Lightning Source LLC
Chambersburg PA
CBHW070240290526
45789CB00004B/1701